HOW TO WRITE A BOOK REPORT

Writing Skills Series

Written by Brenda Vance Rollins, Ed. D.

GRADES 5 - 8

Reading Levels 3 - 4

Classroom Complete Press
P.O. Box 19729
San Diego, CA 92159
Tel: 1-800-663-3609 | Fax: 1-800-663-3608
Email: service@classroomcompletepress.com

www.classroomcompletepress.com

ISBN-13: 978-1-55319-393-7

ISBN – 10: 1-55319-393-8

Critical Thinking Skills

How to Write a Book Report

Level	Skills For Critical Thinking	1	2	3	4	5	6	7	8	9	10	11	12
LEVEL 1 Remembering	• Define, Describe, Identify, Label, List, Match, Name, State	✓	✓	✓	✓	✓	✓	✓	✓	✓	✓	✓	✓
LEVEL 2 Understanding	• Describe, Discuss, Explain, Paraphrase, Restate, Summarize	✓	✓	✓	✓	✓	✓	✓	✓	✓	✓	✓	✓
LEVEL 3 Applying	• Predict, Project, Provide, Relate, Report; Show	✓	✓	✓		✓			✓	✓	✓	✓	
LEVEL 4 Analysing	• Illustrate, Infer, Outline, Point Out, Prioritize, Recognize		✓	✓	✓		✓		✓	✓	✓		
LEVEL 5 Evaluating	• Appraise, Compare and Contrast, Conclude, Decide, Support			✓		✓			✓	✓	✓	✓	
LEVEL 6 Creating	• Categorize, Compare, Compose, Contrast, Create; Design; Revise	✓	✓	✓	✓	✓			✓	✓	✓		✓

Based on Bloom's Taxonomy

Contents

Assessment Rubric

How to Write a Book Report

Student's Name: ______________________ Assignment: ________________ Level: ________

	Level 1	Level 2	Level 3	Level 4
Introduction	No attempt.	1st paragraph: no title, very little description, too much plot.	1st paragraph: includes the book title with a brief description.	1st paragraph: includes title of book, clearly stated main idea including who/what the story is about.
Main Characters	No attempt.	Characters are named.	Main characters are mentioned with plot elements.	Main characters are clearly named and a brief character description is included for each main character.
Setting	No attempt.	Setting is briefly mentioned, either where or when it takes place, but not both.	Setting, when and where is mentioned with little details.	Setting is clearly described with the time the story takes place and where it takes place clearly described.
Problem/Conflict	No attempt.	Problem and Solution are described with minimal details. Difficulty providing information regarding the problem and solution.	Problem is briefly described with 3 major events not specifically described. Solution is present.	Problem is clearly stated and summarized. 3 specific major events are clearly listed and described. Solution to the problem is described concisely.
Final Outcome/ Conclusion	No attempt.	Ending is unclear. No specific details.	Continuation of plot. Somewhat of an ending to the book is present.	How the book ends is clearly stated with details. Clear conclusion of the book with details.
Grammar/ Mechanics	No attempt. Book report is difficult to read and doesn't appear to be proofread very carefully or not at all.	Book report contains between 10-15 errors in punctuation, spelling, and grammar. More effort could have been put into proofreading.	Book report contains 5-10 errors in punctuation, spelling, and grammar.	Book report has been edited and the final copy contains very few errors in punctuation, spelling, and grammar.

STRENGTHS:

WEAKNESSES:

NEXT STEPS:

Teacher Guide

Our resource has been created for ease of use by both TEACHERS and STUDENTS alike.

Introduction

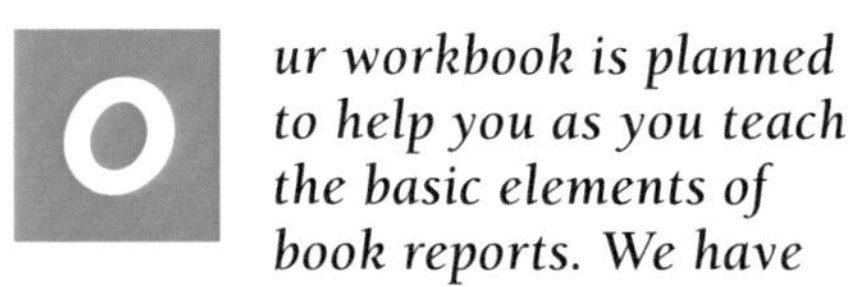

Our workbook is planned to help you as you teach the basic elements of book reports. We have included the required and other numerous details for describing the elements of good book reports, as well as the steps that students need to take to write them. Also included are many graphic organizers designed to assist your students as they read and conduct research about their books and as they prepare the reports for sharing with an audience.

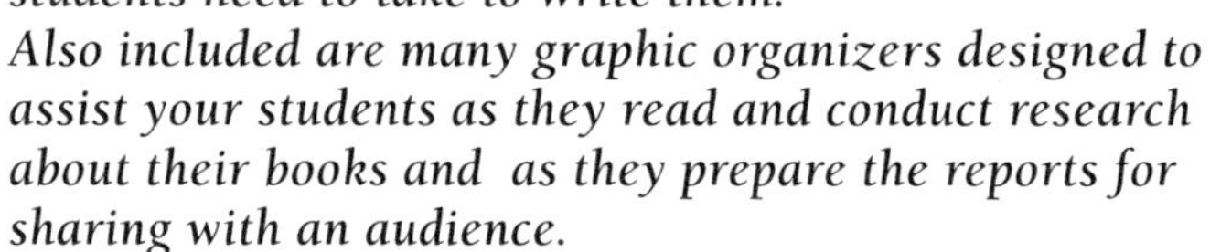

The "Writing Watchdog" emphasizes important concepts throughout the book. Definitions of important terms and many opportunities to practice the skills being taught also make this book user-friendly and easy to understand. In addition, the objectives used in this book are structured using Bloom's Taxonomy of Learning to ensure educational appropriateness.

How Is Our Resource Organized?

STUDENT HANDOUTS

Reading passages and **activities** (*in the form of reproducible worksheets*) make up the majority of our resource. The reading passages present important grade-appropriate information and concepts related to the topic. Embedded in each passage are one or more questions that ensure students understand what they have read.

For each reading passage there are **BEFORE YOU READ** activities and **AFTER YOU READ** activities.

- The BEFORE YOU READ activities prepare students for reading by setting a purpose for reading. They stimulate background knowledge and experience, and guide students to make connections between what they know and what they will learn. Important concepts and vocabulary from the chapters are also presented.
- The AFTER YOU READ activities check students' comprehension of the concepts presented in the reading passage and extend their learning. Students are asked to give thoughtful consideration of the reading passage through creative and evaluative short-answer questions, research, and extension activities.

Writing Tasks are included to further develop students' thinking skills and understanding of the concepts. The **Assessment Rubric** (*page 4*) is a useful tool for evaluating students' responses to many of the activities in our resource. The **Comprehension Quiz** (*page 48*) can be used for either a follow-up review or assessment at the completion of the unit.

PICTURE CUES

This resource contains three main types of pages, each with a different purpose and use. A **Picture Cue** at the top of each page shows, at a glance, what the page is for.

Teacher Guide
- Information and tools for the teacher

Student Handout
- Reproducible worksheets and activities

Easy Marking™ Answer Key
- Answers for student activities

EASY MARKING™ ANSWER KEY

Marking students' worksheets is fast and easy with this **Answer Key**. Answers are listed in columns – just line up the column with its corresponding worksheet, as shown, and see how every question matches up with its answer!

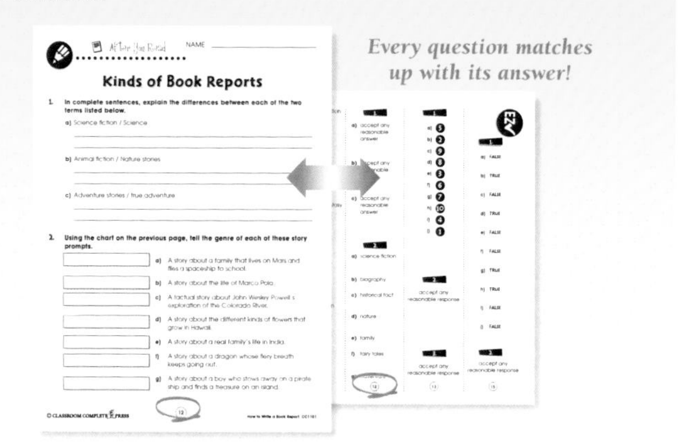

Bloom's Taxonomy* for Reading Comprehension

The activities in this resource engage and build the full range of thinking skills that are essential for students' written composition. Based on the six levels of thinking in Bloom's Taxonomy, assignments are given that challenge students to not only recall what they have read, but move beyond this to understand the text through higher-order thinking. By using higher-order skills of applying, analysing, evaluating, and creating, students become active writers, drawing more meaning from the text, and applying and extending their learning in more sophisticated ways.

This Book Report Writing Kit™, therefore, is an effective tool for any Language Arts program. Whether it is used in whole or in part, or adapted to meet individual student needs, this resource provides teachers with the important questions to ask, inspiring students' interest, creativity, and promoting meaningful learning.

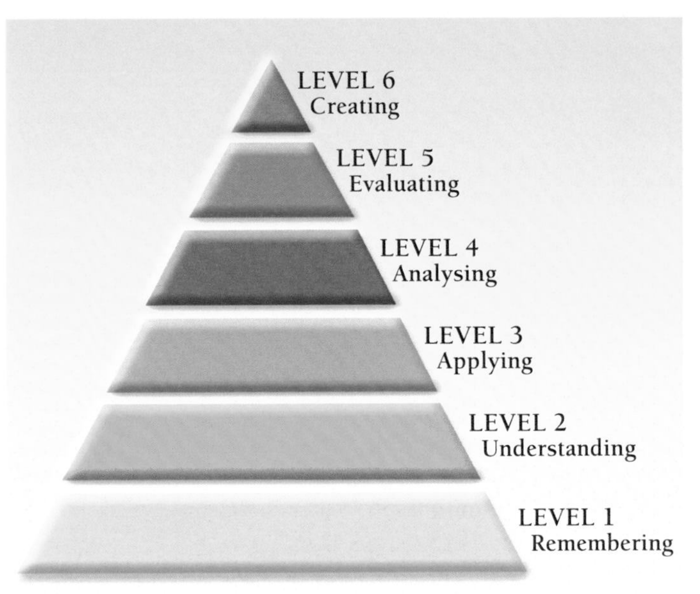

BLOOM'S TAXONOMY*: FOR WRITTEN COMPOSITION

**Bloom's Taxonomy is a widely used tool by educators for classifying learning objectives, and is based on the work of Benjamin Bloom.*

Vocabulary

- **book report** – an essay which gives a brief summary of a book. A book report often includes the reader's reaction to the book.
- **introduction** – the first part of a book report
- **body** – the middle section of a book report in which the main parts of the story are described
- **theme** – the main idea of a story or book • **setting** – the time and place of the story
- **plot** – what happens in the story • **characters** – who the story is about
- **conclusion** – the last part of a book report. The conclusion includes the reader's reaction to the book and recommendations about the book
- **author** – a person who writes a story or book
- **illustrator** – a person who draws or paints pictures that accompany a story or a book
- **genres** – kinds of literature • **fiction** – stories made up by an author
- **nonfiction** – stories or books that are based on real people and facts
- **graphic organizers** – diagrams or drawings which help organize a writer's ideas
- **reading journal** – the place where a reader makes notes about the basic elements of a book as well as writes down questions that may arise during his reading
- **informative books** – nonfiction books that provide useful or interesting information
- **biography** – a nonfiction book about someone's life that is written by another person
- **autobiography** – a nonfiction narrative in which an individual tells his or her own life story
- **oral book report** – a book report that is spoken aloud by the presenter to the audience
- **visual aides** – charts, graphs, or other materials that add meaning to the information being presented in an oral book report
- **quotations** – restatements of comments made by a book character • **proofread** – check for mistakes
- **mechanics** – all the capitalization, spelling, and grammar rules that should be followed in a book report
- **form** – all the elements of a good book report that should be a part of a good book report

NAME: ______________________________

What is a Book Report?

1. Complete each statement by circling the correct term.

a) Writing a ____ ________ is a good way to show how well you understand a book and to tell what you think about it.

research paper   persuasive essay   book report   fiction story

b) The first part of a book report is the ______________.

conclusion   introduction   body   subheading

c) The _______ is the main idea of the book.

characters   theme   setting   plot

d) The _______ is the time and place the story takes place.

characters   theme   setting   plot

e) The _______ is what happens in the story.

characters   theme   setting   plot

f) The __________ are who the story is about.

characters   theme   setting   plot

g) The characters, theme, setting, and plot are all discussed in the _________ part of a book report.

conclusion   introduction   body   subheading

h) In the __________ of the book report you should write how well you liked the book.

conclusion   introduction   body   subheading

i) The person who writes a book is called its __________.

publisher   author   illustrator   reviewer

j) The person who draws pictures for a book is called its __________.

publisher   author   illustrator   reviewer

NAME: ___________________________

What is a Book Report?

While you are a student, you may often be asked to write a report about a book you have recently read. Don't panic! Writing a book report is just another part of the writing process. **A book report is an essay that gives a brief summary of a book and your reaction to it.** Book reports show how well you understood a book and what you think about it. Every book report has the same elements which must be included in order for it to be complete. If you make sure that you include the following things in your book report, an excellent grade should be in your future!

- **Introduction** – the first part of the book report. An introduction should include the **title** (name) and **author** (writer) of the book you read; **why you chose the book**; and **the kind of story the book tells**.
- **Body** – the section of the book report in which you describe the **main parts of a story: theme, plot, setting, and characters**. The **theme** is the main idea of the story. The **setting** is the time and place of the story. The **plot** is what happens in the story. The **Characters** are who the story is about.
- **Conclusion** – this is the summary of your book report. You may want to give your opinion of the book and the most important things you want other people to know about it.

Your teacher may want you to present your book report on a certain form or graphic organizer. You may even be asked to read or tell your book report out loud to your classmates. The rest of this study guide will discuss many kinds of book reports that can be fun for you to write and very interesting for your teacher and classmates to read or hear. So let's get ready to learn about book reports!

The Writing Watch Dog says,
"Remember - every book report has three parts - the introduction, the body, and the summary!"

NAME: ______________________

What is a Book Report?

1. Match each book report term with the correct meaning:

A	book report		the main idea of the book	1
B	introduction		summarizes your thoughts about the book	2
C	theme		who the story is about	3
D	setting		the person who writes a book	4
E	plot		an essay which gives a brief summary of a book and your reaction to it	5
F	characters		the time and place the story takes place	6
G	body		what happens in the story	7
H	conclusion		the first part of a book report	8
I	author		the person who draws pictures for a book	9
J	illustrator		discusses the characters, theme, setting, and plot	10

2. Think about all the different types of books that you have read in the past. Write a well-developed paragraph explaining which type of book is your favorite. The terms in the box below describe some of the different types of books.

fairy tales **mysteries** **science fiction** **everyday life** **historical stories**
adventures **biographies (about people's lives)** **sports** **myths and legends**

____

____

____

____

____

NAME: ____________________

Kinds of Book Reports

Use one of the terms in the box to fill in each blank.

Fiction **nonfiction** **adventure** **historical fiction stories** **family** **historical fact stories** **mystery** **realistic fiction** **science fiction** **science stories** **fairy tales & fantasy** **biographies** **animal storybooks** **nature**

a) All books can be classified as ____________ or ____________.

b) ____________ books are stories that are made up by the author.

c) ____________ books are about real things, people, events, and places.

d) ____________ books are about the environment, taking care of the earth, nature, or wildlife and are fact.

e) ____________ books are about exciting journeys, interesting places, heroes, and spies, and can be fiction or nonfiction.

f) ____________ and ____________ books are about dragons, wizards, imaginary characters and places, and are fiction.

g) ____________ books are about crimes, investigations, puzzles with no answers, and questions about animals or other creatures and can be fiction or nonfiction.

h) ____________ are books about true stories about real people's lives and are fact.

i) ____________ ____________ books are about possible future events, travel to other galaxies, and future inventions and are fiction.

j) ____________ ____________ are books about real life in other times and real people from the past.

The Writing Watch Dog says,
"Genre *means a particular type of literature. All the words in the box above name different genres books for students.*"

NAME: ____________________

Kinds of Book Reports

There are as many kinds of book reports as there are **genres** (jän-rs) or kinds of literature. Each kind should consist of the same three sections – introduction, body, and conclusion. The content of the sections will depend on whether the book is **fiction or nonfiction**.

All books can be divided into two categories – either **fiction** (made up by the author) or **nonfiction** (based on real people and events). In each category there are many types of stories. The chart below shows the major fiction and nonfiction genres:

Fiction

1. **Adventure** – exciting imaginary journeys to interesting places.
2. **Historical Fiction** – stories of imaginary people based upon historical events or made-up stories of real people.
3. **Mystery** – stories about a crime, a question to be answered, or an investigation which are fiction.
4. **Realistic Fiction** - stories that could happen, stories about imaginary families, stories that help us learn about ourselves which are fiction.
5. **Science Fiction** – stories about possible future events, travel to other galaxies, stories about possible future inventions.
6. **Fairytales and Fantasy** – stories about dragons, wizards, imaginary characters and places, magic, heroes, villains, and good vs. evil.
7. **Animal Fiction** - stories about talking animals, animals acting like people, imaginary stories about kids and their pets.

Nonfiction

1. **Adventure** – exciting real journeys to interesting places.
2. **Historical Fiction** – stories about real life in other times or true stories about real people from the past.
3. **Mystery** – stories about a true crime, true puzzles to be solved, or unsolved mysteries.
4. **Families** – real-life families, stories of real people in real situations, multicultural families.
5. **Science** – stories about scientific discoveries and inventions, information about our bodies, stories about the world and outer space which are fact.
6. **Biographies** – true stories about real people, factual information about famous people, facts about other people's lives.
7. **Nature** - true stories about the environment, taking care of the Earth, books about plants, wildlife books that are factual.

NAME: ______________________

Kinds of Book Reports

1. In complete sentences, explain the differences between each of the two terms listed below.

a) Science fiction / Science

____

____

b) Animal fiction / Nature stories

____

____

c) Adventure stories / true adventure

____

____

2. Using the chart on the previous page, tell the genre of each of these story prompts.

[ ] **a)** A story about a family that lives on Mars and flies a spaceship to school.

[ ] **b)** A story about the life of Marco Polo.

[ ] **c)** A factual story about John Wesley Powell's exploration of the Colorado River.

[ ] **d)** A story about the different kinds of flowers that grow in Hawaii.

[ ] **e)** A story about a real family's life in India.

[ ] **f)** A story about a dragon whose fiery breath keeps going out.

[ ] **g)** A story about a boy who stows away on a pirate ship and finds a treasure on an island.

Before You Write Your Book Report

1. Arrange the following steps in the book report writing process in the order that they should occur by putting 1 by what happens first, etc.

______ **a)** Writing the first draft of the report

______ **b)** Choosing a book to read

______ **c)** Getting a grade on your book report

______ **d)** Presenting your book report

______ **e)** Making notes as you read the book

______ **f)** Proofreading your report

______ **g)** Writing the final draft of your report

______ **h)** Returning your book to the library

______ **i)** Organizing your ideas before you begin to write

______ **j)** Talking to others about the kinds of books they like to read

2. Write a short paragraph about the genre of books that you enjoy reading and tell why you enjoy them. You should give at least two book titles as examples of the kinds of books you like to read.

____

____

____

____

____

3. Name one of your favorite authors:

____

NAME: ______________________

Before You Write Your Book Report

If you want to write a good book report, here are several things you should do before you begin to read your book:

- **Decide which kind of book you want to read.** If your teacher lets you choose a book to report on, spend some time deciding which book it will be. Do you like adventure stories or biographies? Maybe you'd like to read a science fiction story or a fairy tale. If you have a hard time deciding, talk to some of your friends about the kinds of books they like to read. One of them may be able to recommend a great book to you. Other good suggestions of books to read might come from your media specialist, your teacher, or your parents.
- **Get the book and begin reading.** The next step you should take is to get the book you have chosen. You might check it out from your school library or you may have to go to your public library. Some people like to own the books they read, so going to a bookstore or ordering online is also a good choice.
- **Write down your book's title, author, illustrator, and copyright date.** You will need this information in your book report. As you read the book, you should write down the main character's names and anything else you think you'll need when you begin your report.
- **Read the entire book!** Don't skim the pages and don't pretend that you read something that you didn't.
- **Use a graphic organizer to help you organize your ideas before you begin to write.** Later in this workbook you will find graphic organizers that will help you with your prewriting activities.
- **Write a good first draft of your book report.** Be sure to include all the important information that your teacher has talked about. We will look at some great book report forms a bit later in this study.
- **Proofread the first draft of your book report.** Look for any mistakes you might have made.
- **Turn in your finished book report.** This is also a good time to return your book to the library.
- **Get a good grade from your teacher!** Now sit back and enjoy the rewards of all your work!

The Writing Watch Dog says,
"Book reports are a fantastic way to tell what you think about a book you have read. When you write a fully developed book report you show your teacher, classmates, and yourself how well you understood what you read."

Before You Write Your Book Report

1. Circle the word True if the statement is true. Circle the word False if it's false.

a) There's no need to include the book title in your book report.

True **False**

b) A good writer will make notes about a book as he/she reads it.

True **False**

c) Every book report is exactly the same as all the other book reports.

True **False**

d) Using a graphic organizer while you're prewriting your book report is a good idea.

True **False**

e) It is impossible to write a good book report about a nonfiction book.

True **False**

f) Students have thousands of books to choose from every time they make book reports.

True **False**

g) A good book report might make one of your classmates want to read the same book.

True **False**

h) A pubic librarian can give you suggestions of a good book to read and report on.

True **False**

i) Book reports should never be fun to write or read.

True **False**

j) Students must enjoy every book they read while they are in school.

True **False**

2. Use the space below to write at least one paragraph that tells about a book that you've read and would like to write a report about. Try to remember as much about the book as you can, but don't worry if you don't remember everything. This is just a practice assignment. The real book reports will come later!

____

____

____

NAME: ____________________

Using Graphic Organizers for Prewriting

Matching: Draw a line from the graphic organizer to the written description of how it is used.

CHARACTER COMPARISON MAP

	Character 1	Character 2
Attribute 1		
Attribute 2		
Attribute 3		

SEQUENCE CHART

First:
Next:
Next:
Then:

STORY MAP

Setting	Time	Place
Characters		
Problem		
Plot/Event		
Resolution		

1. A graphic organizer that helps you remember all the important facts that should be included in a good book report.

2. A graphic organizer that helps you fully describe each character in the book.

3. A graphic organizer that helps you remember the events of the book in the order they happened.

NAME: ______________________________

Using Graphic Organizers for Prewriting

Graphic organizers can be very helpful in the prewriting process of your book report. **Graphic organizers** are **diagrams or drawings** which help you organize your ideas on paper. Sometimes, you can even present your entire book report in the form of a graphic organizer.

There are three graphic organizers that are especially good for prewriting. They are the **Character Comparison Map**, the **Sequence Chart**, and the **Story Map**. Each helps you include various important types of information in your book report.

The **Character Comparison Map** asks you to list the characters in the book and then describe their **attributes**, or qualities and characteristics. Suppose you were writing a book report for ***Charlotte's Web***. Could you list some of Wilbur's attributes? If you said that Wilbur was loving, kind, friendly, and faithful, you are certainly on the right track! Try to think of some other book characters and then list their main attributes in your head. This is good practice for making book reports. Another way to discuss a character's attributes is to compare them with another character in the book. Now think about Fern in ***Charlotte's Web***. Did she and Wilbur have some of the same attributes? Yes, they surely did!

The **Sequence Chart** gives you an opportunity to list all the important events in a book in the order that they occurred. Almost all book report guidelines ask the writer to include some of the most important events that happened in the story. The Sequence Chart is a good way to organize and remember them.

The **Story Map** is another very good graphic organizer to use when you make a book report. It provides a place for you to list the **setting**, or the time and place of the book, the **characters**, or who the book is about, the **plot**, or what happens in the story, the **problem** the characters have, and the **resolution**, or the solution to the problem. By using these and other good graphic organizers during your prewriting, your book report will be informative and fun for others to read or hear.

The Writing Watch Dog says, *"Using graphic organizers as you prepare your book report will help you identify the main concepts in your book. A graphic organizer lets you describe characters, order events, and highlight plot action."*

NAME: ______________________

Using Graphic Organizers for Prewriting

1. Circle each phrase that correctly completes each statement.

a) ____________ ____________ are diagrams or drawings which help you organize your ideas on paper.

characters in a book   graphic organizers   illustrations

b) A ________________ ________________ gives you an opportunity to list all the important events in a book in the order that they occurred.

Story calendar   author's checklist   Sequence Chart

c) The ________________ in a book are who the book is about.

characters   events   conflicts

d) The ____________ ____________________ is a graphic organizer that helps you list all the important parts of a book.

resolution list   story map   timeline list

e) The __________ of a book is the time and place the book takes place.

copyright date   publisher   setting

2. Label each of the graphic organizers below:

A.

First:
Next:
Next:
Then:

B.

Setting	**Time**	**Place**
Characters		
Problem		
Plot/Event		
Resolution		

NAME: ____________________

How to Write a Fiction Book Report

Put the letter of the correct term beside its definition:

A	fiction		the place where a reader makes notes about the basic elements of his/her book—plot, setting, characters, timeline, etc., as well as writes down questions that arise in the reading	1
B	nonfiction		what happens in a book or story	2
C	genre		who a book or story is about	3
D	reading journal		the time and place of a book or story	4
E	recommendations		a particular type of literature or book	5
F	plot		information that should be included in a reading journal	6
G	setting		novels and stories that describe imaginary people and events made up by the author	7
H	characters		other people's suggestions about good books for you to read	8
I	examples and quotes		rereading and correcting any mistakes you have made in the book report	9
J	proofreading & editing		writings that convey factual information and are not works of the author's imagination	10

The Writing Watch Dog says, ***"These are some great book report tips!"***

Book Report Tips

Get all the information from your teacher.
Find the right book for you.
Give yourself time to read.
Take notes as you read.
Mark important pages and passages.
Make an outline.
Write your first draft.
Proofread and edit.

NAME: ______________________

How to Write a Fiction Book Report

Writing a fiction book report is like writing any other kind of essay. You will go through the same steps: prewriting, drafting, proofreading, revising, and presenting your report. However, you should make sure that you understand what a fiction book is.

There are many different genres, or kinds of books. A **fiction book** is a novel or story that describes **imaginary** people and events made up by the **author**, or the person who wrote the book. All fiction books have **characters** (who the story is about), a **setting** (the time and place the story happens), and **plot** (what happens in the book or story). Be sure to include all of these elements in your fiction book report.

The first step in writing a fiction book report is to **choose the book you want to read** unless your teacher has already assigned a book to you. You can ask your media specialist or teacher for their **recommendations** or suggestions of good books, or you may ask your classmates or friends. After you have considered all the choices, it's up to you to pick a book that you want to write about.

The next step in writing a fiction book report is **reading the book**. It is impossible for you to write a good book report if you've only read parts of the book. Read the book and make notes in a reading journal as you're reading. A **reading journal** is the place where you can write down information about the basic elements of your book—plot, setting, characters, timeline, and any questions that you might have while you are reading.

After you finish reading your book, it's time for you to begin the prewriting process. You may use a graphic organizer to help you keep your ideas in order as you plan your report. Be sure to include your comments or thoughts from your reading journal.

Your teacher will probably assign a form for your book report. Forms are really useful because they help you remember all the things you should include in your report. We will talk about these forms a bit later in this book. When you've finished prewriting, it's time for you to begin your first draft of the book report. After the first draft, you should revise, proofread, and finally, write the final draft of the report. Now you're ready to present your "masterpiece" to your classmates and teacher!

NAME: ____________________

How to Write a Fiction Book Report

1. **Put a check mark (✓) beside the title of each book that you think would be good to read for a fiction book report. You may visit your media center or library to get the answers.**

☐ **a)** ***Bridge to Terabithia*** by Katherine Paterson

☐ **b)** ***A Series of Unfortunate Events*** by Lemon Snicket

☐ **c)** ***Planets*** by Gail Gibbons

☐ **d)** ***A Wrinkle in Time*** by Madeleine L'Engle

☐ **e)** ***Planet Earth Science Fair Projects Using the Moon, Stars, Beach balls, Frisbees and Other Far-out Stuff*** by Robert Gardner.

☐ **f)** ***Harry Potter and the Sorcerer's Stone*** by J.K. Rowling

☐ **g)** ***The Chocolate Touch*** by Patrick Catling

☐ **h)** ***Portraits of African-American Heroes*** by Tonya Bolden

☐ **i)** ***I was a Sixth Grade Alien*** by Bruce Coville

☐ **j)** ***Dragon Rider*** by Cornelia Funke

2. Put an "X" next to the best graphic organizer for a **fiction** book report.

a) ☐

Name ____________________ Date
Title of the Book
____
Author ____________________
1. Is the author an expert on the subject? _____Yes _____No _____Unsure
2. On the back of the title page check for the following information:
Copyright date ____________________
Number of editions ____________________
3. Is the copyright date recent enough to include the newest facts on the topic?
_____Yes _____No _____Unsure
4. Are there pictures and diagrams? _____Yes _____No
If so, are they helpful? _____Yes _____No
5. Is the book convenient to use? Rate the following:
Index: _____Excellent _____Fair _____Not helpful
Table of Contents: _____Excellent _____Fair _____Not helpful
Headings: _____Excellent _____Fair _____Not helpful
Vocabulary in Italics: _____Excellent _____Fair _____Not helpful
6. Does the book cover the topic fully and is the information easy to understand?
Why or why not? ____________________
____
7. What made you select this book as a resource? _____Cover _____Title
_____Other
8. What overall rating would you give this resource?
_____ Use with caution
_____ Good basic information
_____ Excellent for assignment

b) ☐

Book Report
Title____________________
Author____________________
Illustrator____________________
Main Characters____________________
____
____
Setting____________________
Explain the plot of this book____________________
____
____
____
Would you recommend this book to a friend?
Why or why not?
____
____
____
List any other books written by this author.
____
____
____

NAME: ______________________

Graphic Organizers for Fiction Book Reports

Draw a line from each graphic organizer to it's written description.

STORY MAP

Title of Book
Setting
Characters
Problem
Major Events
Conclusion
Recommendation

FICTION BOOK REPORT

This book (title) was written by (author). It was published in (copyright date) by (name of publisher). I obtained the book from (where you got the book).

One important character in the book is (character's name). Physically* this character is (Give a very complete physical description of the character). His/Her personality* could be described as (__________, __________, and _______).

I approve/disapprove of the ending of (book title) because (List your reasons; be specific in your comments). The only change I might want to make in the book is (suggestions? You must suggest changes, even if you did like the book.).

BOOK REPORT FOR INDEPENDENT READING

Title of Book ______________ Author ______________

Setting ______________________________________

Main Characters: Brief description of each character.

1.______________ ____________________________
2.______________ ____________________________
3.______________ ____________________________
4.______________ ____________________________

Summary: Write a summary about the story.

____
____

How did the story end ?(Conclusion)

____

1. A book report form that encourages the writer to compose complete sentences and paragraph describing the book's characters, their problems, and whether or not he/she approves of the ending of the book.

2. A book report form that is designed for the writer to report on books read during independent reading. This form lets the writer describe the main characters and the setting of the book.

3. A book report form that asks only for the basic elements of the book including the major events and the writer's recommendation of the book to other readers.

NAME: ______________________________

Reading Passage 

Graphic Organizers for Fiction Book Reports

You know that a **fiction book** is a novel or story that describes **imaginary** people and events made up by the **author**, or the person who wrote the book. All fiction books have **characters** (who the story is about), a **setting** (the time and place the story happens), and **plot** (what happens in the book or story).

There are many good **graphic organizers** for fiction book reports. Each one includes some or all of the elements of a fiction book. Sometimes, your teacher will tell you which kind of graphic organizer to use when you present your fiction book report, but you will often have the chance to choose your own organizer for your report. When you do get to choose, make sure that the organizer gives you the opportunity to discuss some or all of the elements of fiction.

One very good graphic organizer for fiction books is the **Characterization Organizer**. The reader is asked to "describe one change in the main character's personality from the beginning of the novel to the end of the novel" and "how is the setting important to the development of the plot?" The emphasis on the characters in a book is an excellent way to let others know how much you like or dislike it and whether or not you would recommend it to others.

Another good graphic organizer for a fiction book is the **Comparing Myself to a Character**. The reader is asked to compare three of the main character's traits to three of the reader's own traits. Doing this gives the reader a chance to identify his/her own and the character's likenesses and differences.

The **Story Frame Summary** graphic organizer gives the reader an opportunity to summarize the plot of a fiction book. In it, the reader identifies the problem that must be solved in the story and all the steps the characters took to solve it. It concludes with an explanation of how the story ends.

These are just some of the excellent graphic organizers that can help you present a good fiction book report. Remember, graphic organizers tell you exactly what they do – **organize your ideas**. Use them whenever you can to make sure that you include everything that's important in your report or essay.

The Writing Watch Dog says,
"Knowing the elements of a story will help you understand what is taking place in your book or novel."

NAME: ____________________

Graphic Organizers for Fiction Book Reports

Using the information from fiction books that you have already read, complete the following graphic organizers: Use your own paper if you need more room.

CHARACTERIZATION ORGANIZER

Describe one change in the main character's personality from the beginning of the novel to the end of the novel; ***include examples of what the characters says and does to demonstrate the change***.

____

What has the main character learned about him/herself or others from his/her experiences in the novel; ***include details from the novel to support your response***.

____

Describe the setting in detail and include examples from the text to support your response. How is the setting important to the development of the plot? Describe a challenge faced by a character in the novel and compare it to a similar challenge you faced or someone you know faced. How are the challenges alike and different?

____

COMPARING ME TO A CHARACTER IN A BOOK

Name: ____________________ Date: ____________

Character:	**Me:**
1. ____________	1. ____________
2. ____________	2. ____________
3. ____________	3. ____________

STORY FRAME SUMMARY

Name: ____________________ Date: ____________

Title of story ____________________

In this story, the problem begins when ____________________

After this, ____________________

Next, ____________________

Then, ____________________

The problem is finally solved when ____________________

The story ends ____________________

NAME: ____________________

Non Fiction Book Reports

1. **Identify the location in a nonfiction book report of each element listed below by placing an I (introduction) in front of the elements that are in the introduction, a B (body) in front of the elements in the body of the report, and a C (conclusion) in front of the elements in the conclusion of the book report.**

   Introduction   Body   Conclusion

   - ☐ **a)** Title
   - ☐ **b)** Would you recommend this book to a friend?
   - ☐ **c)** What the book is about.
   - ☐ **d)** a general overview of the author's topic, main points, and argument
   - ☐ **e)** the book's copyright date
   - ☐ **f)** What you want your readers to know about the book.
   - ☐ **g)** genre
   - ☐ **h)** What are the author's qualifications?
   - ☐ **i)** Who published the book?
   - ☐ **j)** What are the book's strengths or weaknesses?

2. **Put an X next to the title of each nonfiction book** (Use your school library if you need to).

   - ☐ **a)** ***The American Story: 100 True Tales from American History*** by Jennifer Armstrong
   - ☐ **b)** ***The Pinballs*** by Betsy Byars
   - ☐ **c)** T***he Red Badge of Courage*** by Stephen Crane
   - ☐ **d)** ***Now Is Your Time! The African-American Struggle for Freedom*** by Walter Dean Myers
   - ☐ **e)** ***1776*** by David McCullough
   - ☐ **f)** ***The Princess Bride*** by William Goldman

NAME: ___________________________

Non Fiction Book Reports

There are some differences between a fiction book report and a nonfiction book report. A **fiction book** is a novel or story that describes **imaginary** people and events made up by the **author**. A **nonfiction book** is about **real things, people, events, and places**. Diaries, letters, and true historical stories are all nonfiction.

A **nonfiction book report** is made up of three parts – the **introduction**, the **body**, and the **conclusion**. The information in each part is described in this diagram:

The introduction of the book report includes:

- The title of the book
- The author of the book
- A brief introduction to the book
- The genre of the book
- The book's copyright and publishing information

The body of the book report includes:

- the subject of the book
- a summary of the book
- The author's qualifications
- Examples from the book
- a general overview of the author's topic, main points, and argument

The conclusion of the book report includes:

- The book's strengths and weaknesses
- Would you recommend this book to a friend?
- What you want your readers to know about this book.

All nonfiction books can be divided into three types: 1. informative, 2. biographies, and 3. autobiographies. Each type of nonfiction book is described in this diagram:

Types of Nonfiction Books

1. **Informative Books** – books that provide useful or interesting information. Informative books include all kinds of textbooks such as science, social studies, and history books.
2. **Biography** – The story of a person's life written, composed, or produced by another person.
3. **Autobiography** - A narrative in which an individual tells his or her own life story.

There are thousands and thousands of nonfiction books in your media center or library. Your media specialist will be glad to help you find the type of nonfiction book you wish to read and make a report about. Of course, you can always find the titles of nonfiction books by using the internet or visiting a bookstore.

NAME: ____________________

Non Fiction Book Reports

1. Identify the type of nonfiction book each title represents by placing an I in front of the informative books, a B in front of the biographies, and an A in front of the autobiographies.

> Keep in mind that **Informative Books** are books that provide useful or interesting information. Informative books include all kinds of textbooks such as science, social studies, and history books. A **Biography** is the story of a person's life written, composed, or produced by another person. And an **Autobiography** is a narrative in which an individual tells his or her own life story.

- ☐ a) ***Maya Angelou: A Song Flung up to Heaven*** by Maya Angelou
- ☐ b) ***The Big Book of Dinosaurs*** by Angela Wilkes
- ☐ c) ***I Had a Hammer: the Hank Aaron Story*** by Hank Aaron
- ☐ d) ***Spiders Spin Webs: And Other Questions about Insects*** by Amanda O'Neill
- ☐ e) ***Rachel: The Story of Rachel Carson*** by Amy Erlich
- ☐ f) ***Founding Father: Rediscovering George Washington*** by Richard Brookhiser
- ☐ g) ***Sacajawea: The Story of Bird Woman and the Lewis and Clark Expedition*** by J. Brouchac
- ☐ h) ***The Titanic*** by Judy Donnelly
- ☐ i) ***First Son: George W. Bush and the Bush Dynasty*** by Bill Minutaglia
- ☐ j) ***Little House in the Big Woods*** by Laura Ingalls Wilder

2. List at least three suggestions of books that you'd like to read under each of the nonfiction headings.

	Informative Books	Biography	Autobiography
a)	______	______	______
b)	______	______	______
c)	______	______	______

NAME: ______________________________

Graphic Organizers for Non Fiction Book Reports

Draw a line from each graphic organizer to it's written description.

A.

Name ____________________ Date ______________
Title of the Book
____
Author ______________________________
1. Is the author an expert on the subject? _____Yes _____No _____Unsure
2. On the back of the title page check for the following information:
Copyright date ______________
Number of editions ______________
3. Is the copyright date recent enough to include the newest facts on the topic?
_____Yes _____No _____Unsure
4. Are there pictures and diagrams? _____Yes _____No
If so, are they helpful? _____Yes _____No
5. Is the book convenient to use? Rate the following:
Index: _____Excellent _____Fair _____Not helpful
Table of Contents: _____Excellent _____Fair _____Not helpful
Headings: _____Excellent _____Fair _____Not helpful
Vocabulary in Italics: _____Excellent _____Fair _____Not helpful
6. Does the book cover the topic fully and is the information easy to understand?
Why or why not? ______________________________
____
7. What made you select this book as a resource? _____Cover _____Title
_____Other
8. What overall rating would you give this resource?
_____ Use with caution
_____ Good basic information
_____ Excellent for assignment

1. A graphic organizer that is used for a person's life story that is written by the person.

B.

2. BOOK REPORT FORM: BIOGRAPHY
Title ______________________________
Author ______________________________
The book is a biography of ______________
______________, *who was born on (birth date)* ______________
in (birthplace) ______________.
Write a summary of what you learned.
____
____
What is the most interesting fact about this person?
____
____
How would you describe this person?
____
____
If you could meet this person what question would you ask him/her?
____
____
Would you recommend this book? Why or Why not?
____
____

2. A graphic organizer used for an informative book report.

C.

3. Autobiography Book Report
Your name: ______________________________
Title ______________________________
Author ______________________________
Birth Date ______________________________
Birth Place ______________________________
This person is important because ______________
Two important facts I learned about this famous person are: ______________
If you could meet this person, what question would you ask him/her? ______________
____

3. A graphic organizer used for a book report about someone's life that Is written by another person.

NAME: ______________________________

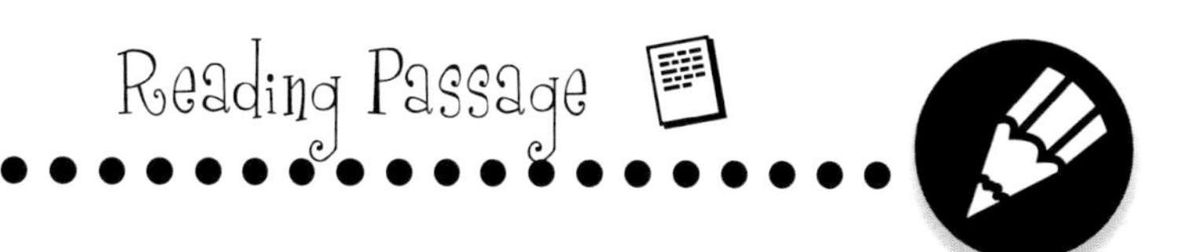

Graphic Organizers for Non Fiction Book Reports

You already know that a **graphic organizer** is a **diagram or drawing** which helps you organize your ideas on paper. There are many graphic organizers that will help you write a book report about a **nonfiction book**.

You also know that a **nonfiction book** is about **real things, people, events, and places** and that **there are three types of nonfiction books - informative books, biographies, and autobiographies**. There are all kinds of informative books. Any book that tells you facts about its subject is an informative book. Therefore, history, science, biology, sociology, economics, animal books, books about snakes and reptiles, and many, many more books are all informative books.

The **Events Chain Graphic Organizer** is a very good tool to use when you want to make a report about a biography or an autobiography. The organizer lists several places for you to describe important events in the life of the person you read about and then gives you a space to write what you've learned from the biography or autobiography.

A **5 W's + H** organizer is another good biography and autobiography organizer. In this form, you write **Who** the book is about, **What** he/she did, **When** it happened, **Where** it happened, and **Why** it happened. The **Five Fingered Organizer** asks the same questions by using the fingers on one hand to stand for each of the 5W's with the H in the palm.

The **Informational Book Report Form** helps you organize all the information that you read in any informational book. The form asks you to describe the type of information the book is about, write some of the interesting facts you learned from the book, tell whether or not you enjoyed reading the book, and if you found it interesting.

A **KWHL Book Report Organizer** is also a good informational book report form. In this organizer, you list what you already **Know** about the book's subject, what you **Want** to learn about the book's subject, **How** you think you will learn this material, and finally, how much you **Learned** from the book when you read it. Of course, in all these organizers you should remember to include the title of the book, the author of the book, the copyright date, and the publisher's name.

NAME: ______________________

Graphic Organizers for Non Fiction Book Reports

Using information from nonfiction books that you have already read, complete each of the graphic organizers below.

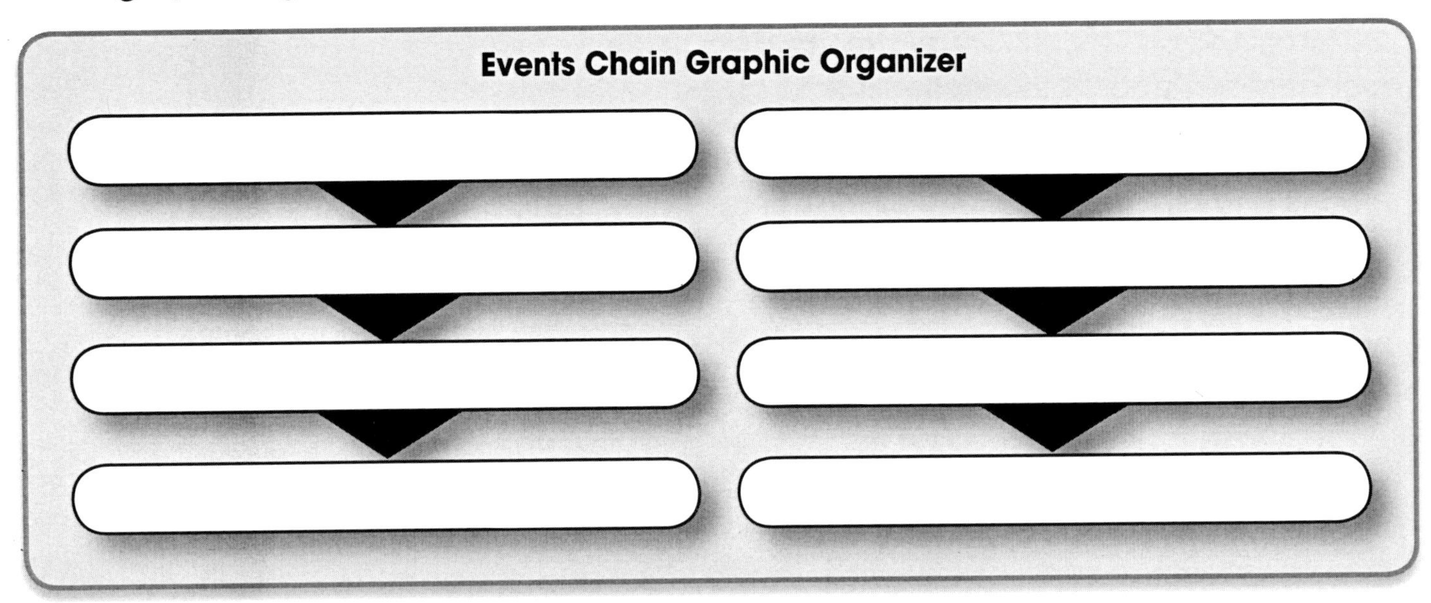

What I Know	What I Want to Know	How I'll Learn It	What I Learned

Title ______________________ Author ______________________

What type of information is this book about? ______________________

Did you find this book interesting? Why or Why Not? ______________________

Write some interesting facts that you have learned. ______________________

Did you like this book? Why or why not? ______________________

NAME: ______________________

Oral Book Reports

1. **Match each term in the box with its correct meaning below.**

Dressing as a book character	**visual aids**	**notes**
audience profile	**rehearse**	**conversational**
pacing	**eye contact**	**transitions**
video	**oral**	

a) ______________ book reports are spoken aloud rather than presented in written form.

b) ________________ means to practice something before presenting or performing it.

c) __________________________ is a brief description that summarizes the characteristics of the people listening to book report.

d) __________________ are the times in an oral book report when the speaker changes from the introduction to the body or from the body to the conclusion of the report.

e) ______________________________ is the act of looking directly into the eyes of another person or group of people.

f) _____________________ are things that the speaker uses in an oral book report to add to its meaning, for example, charts, graphs, or pictures.

g) ________________________ the type of speaking used in oral book reports that is informal in language and style

h) ______________ are something written down, often in a shortened form, as a record or reminder

i) ______________ is something that has been recorded on videotape, especially a movie, music performance, or an oral report.

j) ______________ refers to the speaker's rate or speed of talking

k) ____ is one way to make an oral book report more interesting for your audience.

NAME: ______________________

Oral Book Reports

Many teachers assign at least one **oral book report** to their students each year. An oral book report is spoken aloud by the presenter to the audience. Most oral book reports are from three to five minutes long and are made up of a brief summary of the book, some comments about the characters and plot, and the presenter's opinion of the book. Sometimes, presenters will include **visual aids** in their reports. **Visual aids** are any charts, graphs, drawings, or other materials that will add meaning to the information that is being presented.

An oral book report is not just an essay that is read aloud. It should be an interesting, informative talk or short speech about a book that is meant to entertain your classmates. Your teacher probably won't see your notes or graphic organizer for an oral book report, so it's up to you to do the best job you can as you present your talk to the class. Here are some pointers to help you prepare an excellent oral book report:

Steps to a Great Oral Book Report

1. Make sure that your report has an introduction, a body, and a conclusion. Outline what you are going to say in each section.
2. **Introduction** - use the introduction to tell your audience the general information about your book, such as its title, author, publisher, and year of publication. You may choose to start with an attention-grabber, like a question or a funny story related to the book. Telling it will help you relax and warm your audience to the presentation.
3. **Body** - use the body of your presentation to describe key elements of the story, such as its setting and time period, an overview of the main characters, and a very brief summary of the plot.
4. **Conclusion** - use your conclusion to describe any themes or symbolism in the book and how the author uses them to reinforce important messages. At the end of your presentation, tell your audience what you thought of the book. Would you recommend it? Are you planning to read additional work by this author?

Use these steps to write an outline of what you plan to say in your talk. Your teacher may want you to write your ideas on note cards that you can refer to during the report. Remember, you will be talking to the members of your class, not reading them a story. After you've finished outlining the report, practice several times. The more often you practice, the more at ease you'll become. As you speak, be sure to make **eye-contact** with different members of the audience. Doing this will help your classmates stay focused on what you are saying. Also, try to include one or more **visual aids** such as a chart, picture, map, or even a costume that helps add meaning to your book report. Finally, don't forget to smile as you speak and keep your voice level high enough that everyone can hear you easily.

NAME: ______________________

Oral Book Reports

Fill in the following graphic organizer using information from a book that you have read recently. You may need to visit the media center or use the internet to refresh your memory about your book's details.

Oral Book Report Notes

Author
Title
Publisher
Genre
Main Characters
Setting
Event 1
Event 2
Event 3
Other ideas for oral book reports: **1. Act out a dialog between two of your book's characters.** **2. Act out an interview with the main character of your book.** **3. Act out an interview with the author of your book.** **4. Act out one event that shows the feelings of one of the characters.** **5. Give an oral report and leave off the ending. See if your classmates can guess the ending.**
Conclusion

Oral Book Report Checklist

1. Were my ideas organized clearly?
2. Could my voice be heard easily?
3. Did I read entirely from my notes?
4. Did I include all the important information about the book?
5. Did I maintain good eye contact with my audience?
6. Did I stay focused on the topic?
7. Did I use visual aids that were related to the book's topic?
8. Was my report too long or too short?

NAME: ____________________

Graphic Organizers for Oral Book Reports

Put the letter of the correct term beside the correct meaning:

	Term
A	notes
B	note cards
C	body language
D	transitions
E	outline
F	oral quiz
G	quotation
H	story map
I	sequence map
J	problem/solution map

Letter	Meaning	#
	a listing of all the most important points in a book or story.	1
	a word, phrase, sentence, or group of sentences that relates a preceding topic to a succeeding one or that smoothly connects parts of a speech or piece of writing	2
	a restatement of what a character says in a book or story.	3
	a graphic organizer that lets the presenter list all the elements of a story or book as part of an oral or written book report.	4
	a graphic organizer that lets the presenter list all the conflicts and solutions which occur in a book as part of an oral or written book report.	5
	index cards or similar cards used for recording notes or other information.	6
	a graphic organizer that lets the presenter list all the events in a story or book in the order they occurred as part of an oral or written book report.	7
	a summary of important facts or points written down by a reader or speaker.	8
	gestures, unconscious bodily movements, facial expressions, etc. which serve as nonverbal communication or as accompaniments to speeches or reports.	9
	a short, vocal question and answer session.	10

NAME: ______________________________

Reading Passage 

Graphic Organizers for Oral Book Reports

Keeping all the facts and other things you want to say about your book is very important when you present an oral book report. Graphic organizers are excellent tools to use when you begin to gather the information you plan to use in your report. A very simple and good graphic organizer to use for oral reports is an **outline**, or a listing of all the most important points in a book or story. Many times, speakers write their outlines on **note cards** which are index cards or similar cards used for recording notes or other information. The idea is to use the note cards to help you remember all the key points you want to make in your report. Be sure to practice or rehearse reading these notes before you speak to your class. **Do not read directly from the cards during your talk!**

Other good graphic organizers for oral reports are **story maps, sequence maps, and problem/solution maps**. A **story map** is a graphic organizer that lets the presenter list all the elements of a story or book as part of an oral or written book report. A **sequence map** is a graphic organizer that lets the presenter list all the events in a story or book in the order they occurred as part of an oral or written book report. And a **problem/solution map** is a graphic organizer that lets the presenter list all the conflicts and solutions which occur in a book.

All graphic organizers for oral reports are not the same. Some are designed especially for biographies or autobiographies while others are designed for informational books such as history or science texts. When you want to give an oral report about a fiction book you may want to use an organizer that lets you use **quotations**, or restatements of what a character says.

No matter what kind of book you choose for your report, there are some things that you should remember as you plan for it. Since all book reports have three parts – the introduction, body, and conclusion, be sure to plan what you will say or do as you change or **transition**, from one part to another. You may want to pause briefly, point to your visual aid if you have one, or use other forms of **body language** to show that you are moving from one section to the next. **Body language** consists of any gestures, body movements, or facial expressions which serve as nonverbal communication or as accompaniments to speeches or reports. Most importantly, try to relax and have fun!

The Writing Watch Dog says,
"Oral reports will help you learn how to organize your thoughts and ideas, present them in a sequential order, and to be at ease speaking in front of a group."

NAME: ______________________

Graphic Organizers for Oral Book Reports

Choose a book that you have recently read and use the information from it to complete one of the oral book report graphic organizers below. Make sure that your organizer is suitable for the type of book you choose.

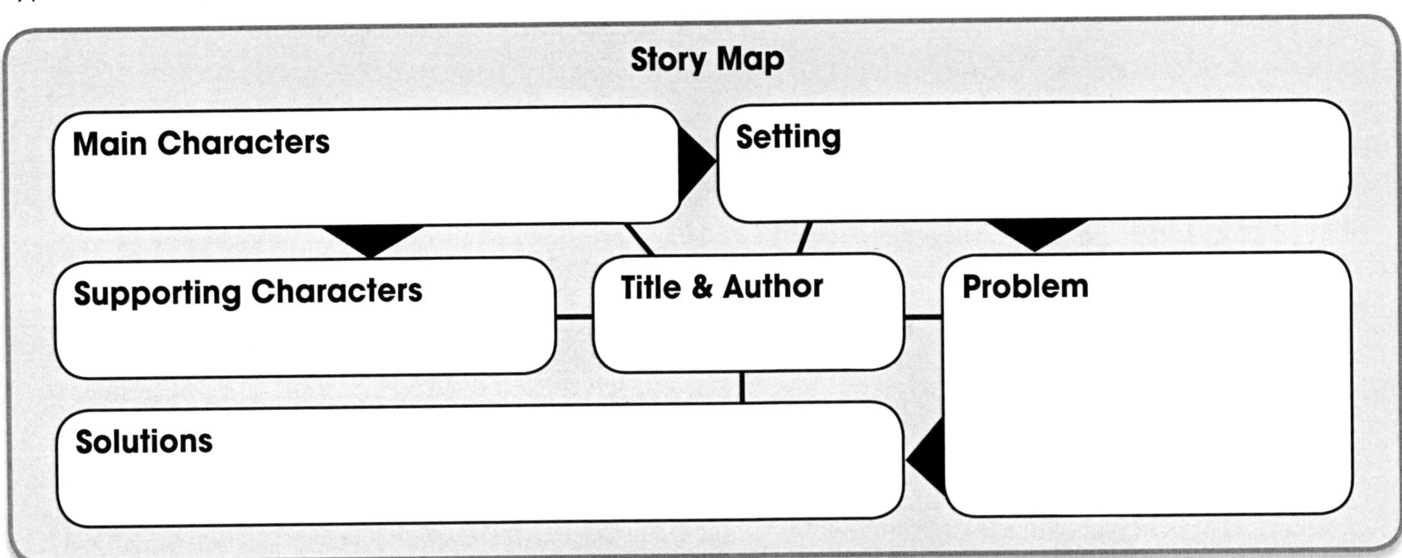

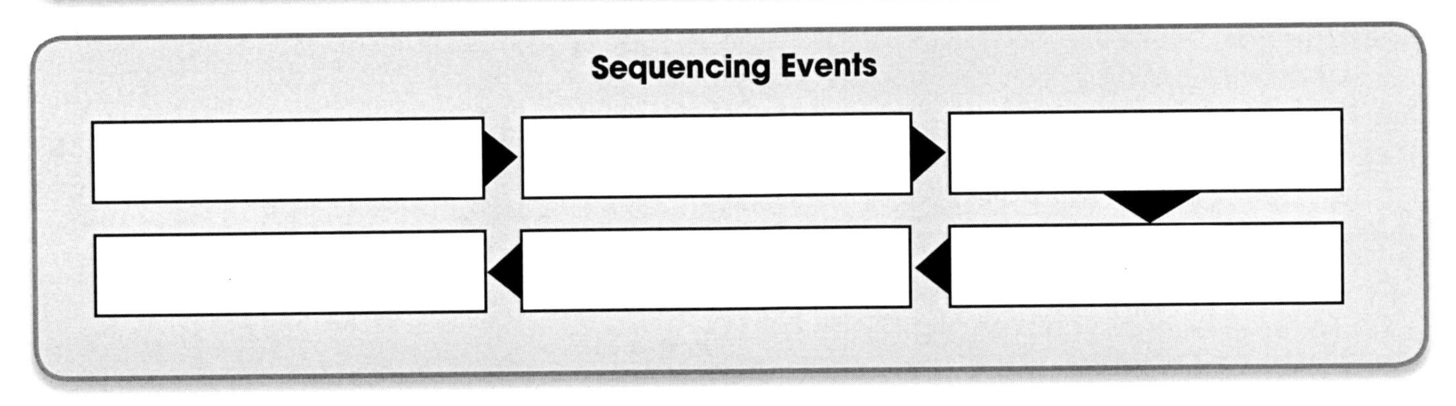

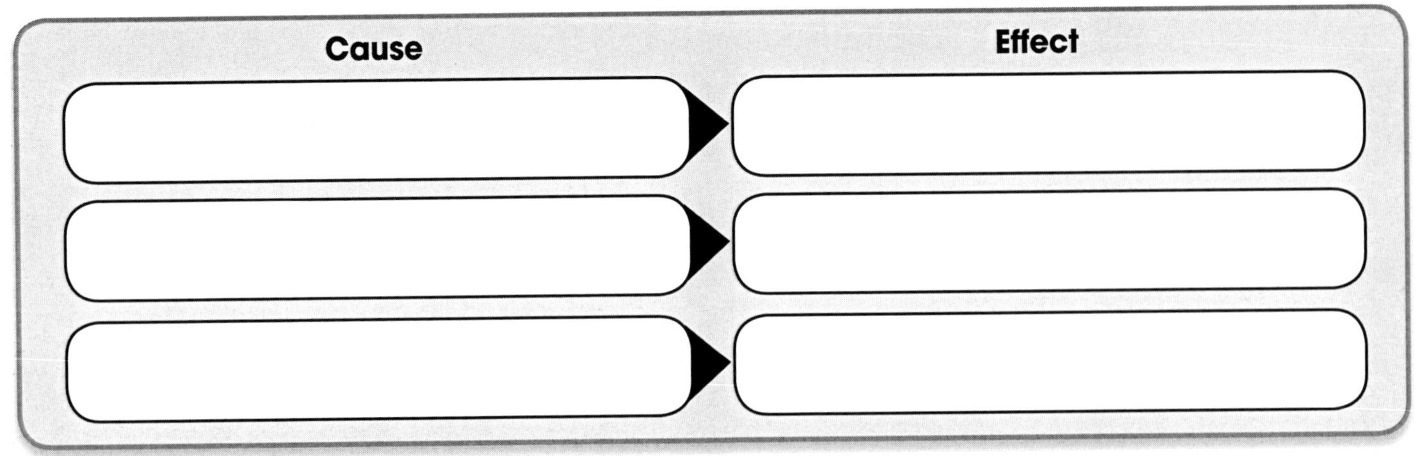

NAME: ______________________________

Proofreading Practice

Fill in each blank with a term from the vocabulary box.

indented	punctuation	character	author	informative	biography	setting
autobiography	proofreading	subject	predicate	quotation marks	capital letter	

a) ______________ means reading a report to look for errors in spelling and composition.

b) Each sentence in a book report must begin with a ____________ ____________.

c) There must be some form of ______________ at the end of each sentence.

d) An incomplete sentence is one that lacks a ______________ or a ______________.

e) Be sure to use ______________ ______________ around the words that are spoken by the characters in the book.

f) The first sentence of each paragraph must be ______________.

g) A person described in a book or play is called a ______________.

h) The person who writes a book is called its ______________.

i) The time and place a story takes place is its ______________.

j) The three main types of nonfiction books are ______________, ______________, and ______________.

Proofreading Checklist

Organization and Content Checklist:

- I used important details.
- When I added details, I didn't wander from the main idea. I remembered my Topic Sentence and the subject of the Writing Prompt and stayed on course.
- I organized my ideas in a logical way.
- My composition answered the question in the prompt.

How's My Style:

- I used many different and descriptive words.
- I used words that helped people see my meaning. They could use all of their senses to feel and even hear my meaning.
- I used different kinds of sentences and didn't start each one with the same word.
- I made every effort to make my writing legible. My spelling and grammar were the very best.

NAME: ______________________________

Proofreading Practice

Now that you have finished preparing your book report it is time to **proofread**, or check it for mistakes. As you proofread, you will be looking at the **mechanics** and the **form** of your book report. The **mechanics** include all the capitalization, spelling, and grammar rules that you should follow while the **form** refers to all the elements of a good book report that must be part of your work.

The first step in proofreading is to let your writing **rest** for a few hours or even a day. Do other things or play a bit before you begin to reread your report. When you do begin to proofread, **read the book report aloud**. Listen to yourself and find if you have left out or added extra words. Do the sentences sound complete? Do all the subjects and predicate agree in tense and number? Are you saying what you meant to say in your report?

Next, reread your report carefully, word-for-word, making sure that you've spelled each word correctly. If a word doesn't appear to be spelled correctly, look it up in a dictionary. Do all the sentences begin with capital letters? Does each sentence have the correct form of punctuation at its end? Have you used descriptive words and varied the length and types of sentences in the book report? Did you **indent** the first line of every paragraph? All of these questions should be answered as you proofread your report.

Now you should check the **form** of your book report. We have learned that there are elements that must be included in any good book report such as: 1. the title of the book, 2. the author of the book, 3. the publication date of the book, 4. the book's setting, 5. the type of book, 6. the characters, 7. the plot, and 8. your thoughts and recommendations about the book. Be sure that your book report has all these elements as you proofread it.

Finally, ask one of your parents or a friend to proofread the book report for you. Another set of eyes can often catch mistakes that you have overlooked. A parent or friend may ask you to explain a sentence or idea that seems unclear. All of this extra checking will help you make an excellent grade on your book report. When you are finished proofreading, it's time to write the final draft of your report. When you feel that it is as good as you can make it, it is time to turn the report in.

NAME: ______________________________

Proofreading Practice

Proofread this book report and circle any mistakes that you find. There are at least 18 mistakes. Then fill in the blanks below with the elements of a good book report from this example. There will be one element missing.

***The Bad Beginning*: A Terrible Tale**

Do you enjoy happy endings. If so, The Bad Beginning by Lemony Snicket is a book you'll want to avoid. This is a storie with a bad begining, a bad midle and a bad ending. why would anyone want to read such a bade book? It's all in good fun!

The bad beginning is a story about the suffering of three orphaned childern at the hands of their uncle, Count Olaf. Although Violet, Klaus, and Sunny are the inheritors of a huge fortune, they cannot claim the money until they are older. for now, they must live with Olaf and cook and clean for him and his terrible theater friends. Why would such a cruel charater take in three orphans? He wants to steel their fortune, of course

I can't tell you how the story ends, but I can tell you what I enjoyed most about the book. Snicket makes his readers laff and want to continue reeding, even in the most terible situations. for example, he constantly warns his reader to put down the book because nothing good could possible come of the orphans' unfortunate situation. He writes: "It is my sad duty to write down these unpleasent tails, but there is nothing stopping you from puting this book down at once..." Of course, Snicket's warnings only made me even more curiosity to find out what would become of the family in the end.

Will Olaf's evel plot win out? Or will these three crafty kids outwit him? If your not afraid of a little misery and a whole lot of mischief, then I recommend you read The Bad Beginning and find out for yourself.

Title ______________________ **Author** ______________________

Publication date ______________________

Characters ______________________

Plot ______________________

Recommendations ______________________

Opinions ______________________

NAME: ______________________

Review to Remember

Answer each question with a complete sentence.

1. **What is a book report?**

   ____

2. **What are the three parts of a good book report?**

   ____

3. **What does genre mean?**

   ____

4. **Into what two categories can all books be divided?**

   ____

5. **What types of information should all good book reports contain?**

   ____

6. **What is an oral book report?**

   ____

7. **How can graphic organizers help you write a good book report?**

   ____

8. **Into which three groups can all nonfiction books be divided?**

   ____

9. **Why is it important to read the entire book you've chosen before you begin to write your report?**

   ____

10. **Write at least three sentences about the book that you plan to use for your book report.**

    ____

    ____

    ____

NAME: ______________________________

Review to Remember

A book report is an essay which gives a brief summary of a book and your reaction to it. Writing a book report is a way to show how well you understand a book and to tell what you think about it. A good book report has three sections: the introduction, the body, and the conclusion.

A book report's introduction must include the title of the book (underlined or typed in italics), the book's author, why you chose the book to make a report, and the book's **genre**, or type of story. The **body** of a book report is the section of the book report in which you describe **the main parts of a story: theme, plot, setting, and characters**. The **theme** is the main idea of the story. The setting is the time and place of the story. The **plot** is what happens in the story. The **characters** are who the story is about. The **conclusion** is the summary of your book report. In it, you will give your opinion of the book and the most important things you want other people to know about it.

All books can be divided into two kinds – **fiction and nonfiction**. Fiction books are made up by the author while nonfiction books are based on real people or events. Nonfiction books can be informative, biographical, or autobiographical. A **biography** is the story of a person's life that is written by someone else. An **autobiography** is the story of a person's life written by that person.

Book reports can be presented in many different ways. Some book reports are written and turned in to the teacher and others are presented orally in front of a group of people. Most book report authors use some kind of **graphic organizer** to help gather and organize the information about the book.

Before beginning a book report it is very important to read the entire book. By doing this you will gain a general understanding of the plot, characters, and organization of the book. Besides, you'd feel very foolish trying to answer questions about the book if you hadn't read all of it! If you have a choice about the book to make a report on, be sure to choose one that sounds like it would be interesting to you. Then, as you read, make notes about the characters, plot, setting, and other important parts of the book.

The Writing Watch Dog says,
"Make sure that you choose a book that interests you, take notes while you read it, and then write a great book report to share the book with your friends and classmates. You will have a great sense of accomplishment when you're finished."

NAME: ______________________________

Review to Remember

1. Circle the word True if the statement is true. Circle the word False if it's false.

a) There are only three types of graphic organizers suitable for book reports.

True **False**

b) Writing a book report is a good way to show that you understand the book.

True **False**

c) A book's author is the person who wrote the book.

True **False**

d) The setting of a book is the shelf it is stored on in the library or media center.

True **False**

e) Some students get nervous before giving an oral book report.

True **False**

f) All nonfiction books can be divided into four groups.

True **False**

g) It is very important to read the whole book before you begin to make a report on it.

True **False**

h) You can write another person's autobiography.

True **False**

i) Nonfiction books are based on the stories of real people and places.

True **False**

j) The characters in a book are not important in the book report.

True **False**

2. Put these steps of writing a good book report in order by placing 1 next to what happens first, 2 next to what happens second, etc..

_____ **a)** write the report

_____ **b)** read the book

_____ **c)** use a graphic organizer to gather information about the book.

You have spent a great deal of time writing book reports. Now let's write to the author of one of your favorite books!

On your computer, go to http://falcon.jmu.edu/~ramseyil/biochildhome.htm . There you will find several choices beginning with "Print bibliographies" and continuing to all the letters of the alphabet. Choose a letter and click on it. Here you will find many children's authors listed. Click on any name that is followed by "teacher resource file" and read about that author. When you have finished, write the rough draft below of an e-mail that you'd like to send to this author. Be sure to ask questions about their books and characters.

Choose a favorite character from a book you have read.
Now pretend that you and this character can go on a five-day vacation together.
Write a diary entry for each day describing the events of each day.
You may use additional paper from your notebook if you like.

Writing Task # 3

Imagine that your teacher has asked you to write the story of your own life – your autobiography. Make an outline and then write the first two paragraphs of your autobiography below. Be sure to make it interesting for your readers.

Writing Task # 4

Choose one book that you have read recently.
Now pretend that your job is to design a TV commercial advertising this book.
Write the script for the commercial and draw the cover of the book that you will be advertising.
Remember to include the book title, author, where it is sold, and how much it costs in the script.

Writing Task #5

Using your computer, go to http://www.ncsu.edu/globalbookclub/books.html
You will see months of the year followed by different book genres. Choose the type of book that you'd like to read about and click on it. You will see the titles of books that have been reviewed on this site. Choose one of the book reviews and read it carefully. Then write a review of the review. Tell if you think the author of the review covered all the important points about the book. Have you ever read this book? Does this review make you want to read it? What grade would you give the author of the book review?

____

____

____

____

____

____

____

Choose a favorite book you've already read and check it out of your library again. You learned that quotations from the book are great to use in book reports. Browse through your book and write down some of your favorite quotes from it. Try to get at least two quotes from each character. Remember to identify who is speaking, the title of the book, and the page from which the quote is taken. Always set aside the actual words the character says with quotation marks.

____

____

____

____

____

____

NAME: ______________________

Crossword

Word List

biography
body
book report
characters
fantasy
genres
informative
introduction
mystery
organizer
quotes
setting
theme
title
visual

Across

3. A true story about a real person's life that is written by another person
4. The time and place of a story or book
8. ____________ Aids are often used in oral book reports
9. The first section of a book report
10. The main idea of a story or book
12. Graphic ____________
13. A story about a crime, or an investigation
14. The name of a book
15. Kinds or types of books or stories

Down

1. The middle section of a book report
2. Who the book or story is about
5. One type of nonfiction book
6. Actual words spoken by a character in a book or story
7. An essay which gives a brief summary of a book
11. A story about imaginary characters or places

NAME: ______________________________

Word Search

Find the following key words from the story. The words are written horizontally, vertically, diagonally and some are even backwards.

author	fiction	nonfiction	quotations
body	genres	oral	setting
biography	graphic	organizers	theme
book report	introduction	plot	visual aids
conclusion	journal	proofread	

b	o	o	k	r	e	p	o	r	t	j	p	w	h	e
b	t	r	g	p	n	l	w	x	u	h	o	d	m	l
i	g	g	c	r	w	o	j	y	t	u	e	s	d	a
o	r	a	l	o	k	t	n	e	w	n	b	m	l	a
g	a	n	t	o	j	q	o	h	k	e	n	b	e	m
r	p	i	c	f	m	f	i	c	t	i	o	n	s	s
a	h	z	e	r	i	t	t	k	s	d	n	z	e	d
p	i	e	j	e	g	i	c	e	y	u	f	f	r	i
h	c	r	l	a	n	r	u	o	j	e	i	j	n	a
y	d	s	g	d	t	u	d	e	c	r	c	n	e	l
s	n	o	i	t	a	t	o	u	q	o	t	e	g	a
s	e	t	t	i	n	g	r	o	f	h	i	c	u	u
e	b	m	y	l	i	q	t	y	d	t	o	j	g	s
v	q	w	x	e	t	o	n	n	f	u	n	g	q	i
c	o	n	c	l	u	s	i	o	n	a	e	y	e	v

After You Read

NAME: ____________________

Comprehension Quiz

Answer each question with one or more complete sentences.

5

1. **What is one way to show how well you understand a book and to tell what you think about it?**

____

2. **What are the three main parts of a good book report?**

____

3. **What is a book report?**

____

4. **All books can be divided into two kinds. What are they?**

____

5. **Describe or draw one kind of graphic organizer that would be good to use during the prewriting phase of composing a book report.**

____

6. **Circle the word True if the statement is true. Circle the word False if it's false.**

a) An adventure book can be fiction or nonfiction. **True** **False**

b) Mysteries are always fiction books. **True** **False**

c) Fairy tales and fantasies are nonfiction books. **True** **False**

d) Biographies are always nonfiction books. **True** **False**

e) Some science stories can be fiction. **True** **False**

f) There are two kinds of historical stories – historical fact and historical fiction.
True **False**

g) Body language is important when you're presenting an oral book report.
True **False**

h) Myths and legends are not good subjects for book reports.
True **False**

i) There are many kinds of good graphic organizers to use when you write book reports.
True **False**

9

SUBTOTAL: /14

NAME: ___________________________

Comprehension Quiz

7. Complete each statement by circling the correct term. 5

a) Which part of a book report should include the title (name) and author (writer) of the book you read; why you chose the book; and the kind of story the book tells?

introduction   body   conclusion

b) Which part of a book report is the summary of your book report?

introduction   body   conclusion

c) Which part of a book report is the section in which you describe the main parts of a story: theme, plot, setting, and characters?

introduction   body   conclusion

d) What kind of graphic organizer gives you an opportunity to list all the important events in a book in the order that they occurred?

Cause and Effect Map   Sequence Chart   Characterization Comparison Map

e) What term means "all the elements that must be included in any good book report"?

Visual aids   mechanics   form

8. Write at least one well-developed paragraph describing all the elements of a good book report. 5

____

____

____

____

____

____

____

SUBTOTAL: /10

EZ✓

1.

a) book report
b) introduction
c) theme
d) setting
e) plot
f) characters
g) body
h) conclusion
i) author
j) illustrator

(7)

1.

1 C
2 H
3 F
4 I
5 A
6 D
7 E
8 B
9 J
10 G

2.

Answers will vary

(9)

a) fiction, nonfiction
b) fiction
c) nonfiction
d) nature
e) adventure
f) fairy tales, fantasy
g) mystery
h) biographies
i) science fiction
j) historical fact stories

(10)

1.

a) accept any reasonable answer
b) accept any reasonable answer
c) accept any reasonable answer

2.

a) science fiction
b) biography
c) historical fact
d) nature
e) family
f) fairy tales
g) adventure

(12)

1.

a) 5
b) 2
c) 9
d) 8
e) 3
f) 6
g) 7
h) 10
i) 4
j) 1

2.

accept any reasonable response

3.

accept any reasonable response

(13)

1.

a) **FALSE**
b) **TRUE**
c) **FALSE**
d) **TRUE**
e) **FALSE**
f) **FALSE**
g) **TRUE**
h) **TRUE**
i) **FALSE**
j) **FALSE**

2.

accept any reasonable response

(15)

1. Story Map
2. Character Comparison Map
3. Sequence Chart

(16)

1.

a) graphic organizers

b) sequence chart

c) characters

d) story map

e) copyright date

2.

a) Sequence Chart

b) Story Map

(18)

1 D

2 F

3 H

4 G

5 C

6 I

7 A

8 E

9 J

10 B

(19)

1.

a), b), d), f), h) & j)

2.

b)

(21)

1. Fiction Book Report
2. Book Report for Independent Reading
3. Story Map

(22)

1.

accept any reasonable response

2.

accept any reasonable response

3.

accept any reasonable response

(24)

1.

a) I

b) C

c) B

d) B

e) I

f) B

g) I

h) B

i) I

j) C

2.

a), d) and e)

(25)

EZ✓

1.

a) A
b) I
c) A
d) I
e) B
f) B
g) B
h) I
i) B
j) A

2.

accept any reasonable response

(27)

1. C

2. A

3. B

(28)

accept any reasonable answers

(30)

1.

a) oral
b) rehearse
c) audience profile
d) transitions
e) eye contact
f) visual aids
g) conversational
h) notes
i) video
j) pacing
k) dressing as a book character

(31)

accept any reasonable answers

(33)

EZ✓

1 E
2 D
3 G
4 H
5 J
6 B
7 I
8 A
9 C
10 F

(34)

36

accept any reasonable answers

37

a) proofreading

b) capital letter

c) punctuation

d) subject, predicate

e) quotation marks

f) indented

g) character

h) author

i) setting

j) informative, biography, autobiography

39

Do you enjoy happy endings? If so, The Bad Beginning by Lemony Snicket is a book you'll want to avoid. This is a story with a bad beginning, a bad middle and a bad ending. Why would anyone want to read such a bad book? It's all in good fun!

The Bad Beginning is a story about the suffering of three orphaned children at the hands of their uncle, Count Olaf. Although Violet, Klaus, and Sunny are the inheritors of a huge fortune, they cannot claim the money until they are older. For now, they must live with Olaf and cook and clean for him and his terrible theater friends. Why would such a cruel character take in three orphans? He wants to steal their fortune, of course.

I can't tell you how the story ends, but I can tell you what I enjoyed most about the book. Snicket makes his readers laugh and want to continue reading, even in the most terrible situations. For example, he constantly warns his reader to put down the book because nothing good could possibly come of the orphans' unfortunate situation. He writes: "It is my sad duty to write down these unpleasant tales, but there is nothing stopping you from putting this book down at once…" Of course, Snicket's warnings only made me even more curious to find out what would become of the family in the end.

Will Olaf's evil plot win out? Or will these three crafty kids outwit him? If you're not afraid of a little misery and a whole lot of mischief, then I recommend you read The Bad Beginning and find out for yourself.

40

accept any reasonable responses

42

1.

a) **FALSE**

b) **TRUE**

c) **TRUE**

d) **FALSE**

e) **TRUE**

f) **FALSE**

g) **TRUE**

h) **FALSE**

i) **TRUE**

j) **FALSE**

2.

a) **3**

b) **1**

c) **2**

EZ✓

Across

3. biography
4. setting
8. Visual
9. introduction
10. theme
12. organizer
13. mystery
14. title
15. genres

Down

1. body
2. characters
5. informative
6. quotes
7. book report
11. fantasy

Word Search Answers

b	o	o	k	r	e	p	o	r	t	j	p	w	h	e
b	t	r	g	p	n	l	w	x	u	h	o	d	m	l
i	g	g	c	r	w	o	j	y	t	u	e	s	d	a
o	r	a	l	o	k	t	n	e	w	n	b	m	l	a
g	a	n	t	o	j	q	o	h	k	e	n	b	e	m
r	p	i	c	f	m	f	i	c	t	i	o	n	s	s
a	h	z	e	r	i	t	t	k	s	d	n	z	e	d
p	i	e	j	e	g	i	c	e	y	u	f	f	r	i
h	c	r	l	a	n	r	u	o	j	e	i	j	n	a
y	d	s	g	d	t	u	d	e	c	r	c	n	e	l
s	n	o	i	t	a	t	o	u	q	o	t	e	g	a
s	e	t	t	i	n	g	r	o	f	h	i	c	u	u
e	b	m	y	l	i	q	t	y	d	t	o	j	g	s
v	q	w	x	e	t	o	n	n	f	u	n	g	q	i
c	o	n	c	l	u	s	i	o	n	a	e	y	e	v

1. Accept any reasonable answer

2. Accept any reasonable answer

3. Accept any reasonable answer

4. Accept any reasonable answer

5. Accept any reasonable answer

6.

a) TRUE
b) FALSE
c) FALSE
d) TRUE
e) TRUE
f) TRUE
g) FALSE
h) FALSE
i) TRUE

7.

a) introduction

b) conclusion

c) body

d) sequence chart

e) form

8. Accept any reasonable reply

Author's Biographical Information

This graphic organizer is a good research tool for students to use.
If they use this organizer to gather information about their favorite author's life, they will have a little something "extra" to include in their book reports.

Student name: ________________________________

Author's name: ________________________________

Date of Birth: ________________________________

Place of Birth: ________________________________

Where he/ she lives now: ________________________________

Title and Date of book published: ________________________________

____

Additional Interesting Information about the Author: ____________

____

____

____

Other Books by this Author: ________________________________

____

____

My Evaluation of this Book: ________________________________

____

____

____

Sources of Information: ________________________________

____

Fiction Book Characterization Organizer

This is a graphic organizer that is designed to be used during the research phase of a student's book report project. If you want to encourage your students to pay special attention to the author's methods of characterization in their books, give each one of them a copy of this organizer. It gives just enough direction to enable them to recognize the importance of characterization and setting in a good fiction novel.

First and Last name: ______________________________

Date: ______________________________

Title of Book: ______________________________

Author: ______________________________

Describe one change in the main character's personality from the beginning of the novel to the end of the novel; ***include examples of what the character says and does to demonstrate the change***: ______________________________

____

____

____

What has the main character learned about him/herself or others from his/her experiences in the novel? ***Include details from the novel to support your response.***

____

____

____

Describe the setting in detail and include examples from the text to support your response. How is the setting important to the development of the plot? Describe a challenge faced by a character in the novel and compare it to a similar challenge you faced or someone you know faced. How are the challenges alike and different?

____

____

____

Book Report Graphic Organizer

1st paragraph Author, Setting, Time (setting is where and when the story took place)

____

____

____

2nd paragraph Description of Main Characters

____

____

____

____

3rd paragraph Problem/Solution Faced by Characters

____

____

____

____

4th paragraph Theme/Moral (underlying idea & subject/lesson learned)

____

____

____

____

5th paragraph Opinion/Recommendation (What did you think of this book? Who would you tell to read it?)

____

____

____

Fiction Book Report Prewriting

Write the title and author of your book in the orange box.
Write the theme of the book in the green one.
Use the balloons to record the names and descriptions of each of the characters.

My Fiction Book Report

This organizer is an attractive way to display fiction book reports in the classroom. Students should be encouraged to personalize the forms as much as they wish.

Name: ____________________

Book Title: ____________________

Author: ____________________

Character Analysis

Main Characters	Description

Summary

Recommendation

Biography Research Page

This is a biography of: ______________________

Date of Birth: ______________________

Place of Birth: ______________________

Three questions I would like to research:

1. ______________________
2. ______________________
3. ______________________

Notes (write keywords and facts)

Write the sources of your information:

1. ______________________
2. ______________________
3. ______________________